september years

caley dent

september years

selected poems
2010–2019

First published in 2019 by Hillside Studios
In association with DIY Publishing Ltd

© Caley Dent
ISBN 978-0-473-49041-6
caleydentauthor@gmail.com

Cover photograph by Caley Dent

Contents

Everything's at ease.

ancient body, standing guard
voice is whispered, throat is dry
cracked skin, deeply scarred
arms forever reach, toward the sky

in your garden, a seat of stone
nearby water, snakes with its flow
a blackbird searches, fallen leaves alone
shattered sun drips, shimmer and glow

two lone souls meet, a spark ignites
never before, have you seen
eternal love, never to blight
what is to come, from what has been

to orbit you, everything's at ease
housed under your, emerald canopy
lavender blooms, on the gentle breeze
complete circle, joined in harmony

Knowing you are near.

vessels are charged
step into phase
skin is elevating

knowing you are near
the air is still
fragrant emanating

clouded sense of ease
the lungs exchange
fuse with this moment

Inside this courtyard.

gentle step and cautious movement
holding the flame
follow the rhythm
of the pulse

beauty and warmth
explore
reach out
in this cool summer night

among the shadow
faces flicker
oblivious and blind
just how they gather

can you see
free of the circle
I am held
by your every motion

the hour is late
our shadow cast long
parallel
over these old tired bricks

the candle is snuffed out
inside this courtyard
left to wonder
only smoke abides

The shore line.

every memory imprinted
across this molecular body
the shore line divides
coarse and abrasive
the foundation endures
step through the surfaces
cool welcoming embrace
holding your breath
clarity is fragmented
looking into the crystal
I can see the moons want
it drags it wrinkles
a static silence is screaming
rushing aloud with its rhythmic beat
distorting my vision
with a cloudy renewal
salt burning the senses
no longer the point of focus
hand about futile protection
writhe in light blisters
harbour your thoughts
entrusted to bubbles
in turn as each inflates
return as you wish
the periodic existence

City lights.

perched upon pole, everyone alive
a cold night, turned warm and inviting
watching the dance, burn through the hours
dissipate breath, join in the glimmer
unfocussed, awoken with cold touch
all awhile, separated by glass

5:29am

Awake

Greedily swallowing away the remaining seconds

10,
    9,
       8,
          7,
             6,
                5,
                   4,
                      3,
                         2,

                                 breath in,
                                     pause,

                SCREAM

Thrown into my bed.
The sandpaper drags over my eyes as they
gradually open,
to burn with the morning light cutting across my
bedroom
where the curtains don't quite meet.

I hit snooze.

The setting sky.

ritual survival of the honest
one leaves the chamber and I am happy
silver dollar stain on the setting sky
kill the essence and start anew condemn
to memory the sixth generation
forget the moon submerging in pink
infantile steps this shell discarded
cooling forgiveness flows still inertia
infinite eyes reflect well of water
soloist echoes masses take courage
red rain smears and the horizon is warm

How much weight in the shadow of time past.

Driven.

15

this blank existence
define the tool
there will be no quarter
grain divides under pressure
driven with reason
you will pay with lead
panic stricken what's my purpose
hold some form of substance
articulate this manifestation
now believed altered
this paper existence

I am.

i am
lotus
i am
breath
my root grounded and nature returns
shaded visit a suns relief
pure echoes for the amenable listen
quiet reflection within binding lattice
i am
one
i am
nothing

Waiting.

moonlit calling
below star dusted velvet
valley carries yearnings
over silverlit dew
ruffle of feathers
a still mind deepens
waiting through purgatory
the sentient watches

I wish you could hear.

you bathe in the light
show your skin off
it is a life source
do not deny it
something is flowing
unveiled warmth
easy to behold
heavy on the heart
smile and collect
coin from the crowd
no longer having
taste for cold meat
I wish you could hear
when I speak true
we shed our skin
inside this realm
twin flames burning
wrapped in one another
we defy decay
it is my fault
I believed in you
do not act like
everything is new
gladly I'd remove
a piece of myself
and I go numb with
would you have me

In my hand.

something caught my eye
I picked it up
my eye was caught

it was the world
all the world in my hand
I held no value

I threw in my hand
God forbid
I should be loved

so I threw it
the tiny sphere
thrown it all away

Footsteps.

light and stretching out shadow
unnoticed taken leave
were you ever really there
leaving only footsteps
soon they too disappear
the air is crisp
chill reaches inside
breath hangs on
life in midair
prisms bend
softening textures
all around
sky is gently falling
distant voices muffled
you do not want to hear
the horizon is lost
if you choose to see
why doesn't anybody else
venture out this far
assuring yourself
footing is stable
as spider webs appear

Hammer on steel.

I see naught for my glowing coals
feed them and keep the oxygen pure I must
commit now to the survival
the work is ceaseless just as my foes
ever prepared it is my burden to bare
link after link this mail grows stronger
all who stand to appose me are glass
the outside worn and renewed within
details lost to memory
my hammer the pressure my head the pounding
every word repeated scenario
the air vibrates with hammer on steel
adding a new ring to each
word and sword fail to penetrate
layered so thick not even light can reach me
my sphere is safe and I can see no flaw

Petals.

along the path
have I collected
these faded petals
carried in crystal
each a delicate reminder
to bring me to my knees
only on occasion
do I look inside
knowing the secret
in the mist
gentle fragrance
of days gone by
blending pastels
I trace each form
not a vein do I miss
illuminating soft light
calling me on
and I have found another

I love you all the same.

entering in poltergeist
you remain unmoved
the great deceiver
I spin the lie
you never picked up
constant screaming
behind bones
you sit in shallow glow
ever stranger never better
I'll start where you won't
take care for me
the back of your neck doesn't listen
I dropped my eyes
why make a sound
I love you all the same
what endures this belligerence

Absorbed.

seemingly random
jewel of the wall
miles traversed
porcelain white pallid
light eddies swirl
softening with salt
crooked spine submerged
pearlescent reflection
warming the core
bathe in the undercurrent
mechanism obsolescent
absorbed in the lather

The station.

all the crowded tracks
echo through the station
and still I wait for you
so we may reach our destination
soles on the pavement
drum into me
I caught myself
a warble in the glass
as this train passes me by
nobody seemed to notice
just another figment
of my imagination
the gust of wind
reshuffles all the dirt
soon something must be due

To see you.

I got your call this morning,
early but you were awake and the day was
nice.

Your voice happy and clear,
I did not mind being awoken.

You had decided we should go out.

The bees are working hard in the daisies that
brush against me.
I hope I look ok, I had rushed to see you.

I saw the net curtain flutter as I walked your
garden path, you must have been watching.

Turning the corner, here you are sunning
yourself in the open doorway.

I run the last few steps to greet you,
you pull me and hold me close.

You are almost ready and won't be long.

I follow to your bedroom,
you are sitting cross legged at the head of your
bed.

Head bowed and eyes low I look to you as I
find a place.
You look up at me with an internal smile,
only just visible.

A small book and pen busily working,
I don't break your concentration.

I don't think you have been up long,
feeling the warmth from your sheets.

Privileged to be here in this sun lit room.

Waiting my eyes rest on your thigh,
I do not dare lay down my head from fear of
being kicked off the bed.

Your hand finds me,
reassuring us both that I am here.

Closing the book,
you get up to slip on your shoes and check
yourself in the mirror.

It's time we were off and you latch the door
behind.

I follow your lead.

The car.

as soon as you got in
eyes clear and bright
the sun is warm inside the car
our conversation is shy
you play with your hair
everything passing as a blur
I think that you are smiling
your trust is with me
the gentle rise and fall of your chest
it feels good to have you near
just us two above the rolling wheels

Drift away.

you filled my eyes
and the world is diminished

there is no cause
and I know my tarnished heart

what could I say
and so the line is laid down

relief of these hands
and we can now drift away

Did you.

did you notice
a sweet gentle pink
quiet scent in the street

did you see
a pure little heart
protected wreathed in thorns

did you stop
petal on your lip
behind ribs picket white

did you care
to be enlivened
was it just a garden rose

Table for two.

come to the table
a table set for two
taking a seat
against my reflection
looking across
steam ardently rises
from the stained pale cup
seeing it's instant
I don't understand
why you're even talking
so far away
well out of arms reach
with cup left half empty
you're already through
before the whitewash of people
I slide in my chair
leaving the cup half full
you may return to

In the forest.

dry autumn leaves felt underfoot
an assembly of the people
with the arrival of dusk
families being torn
crooked fingers all pointed
now starts a trial of innocence
pentacle set in the forest
cool night air is crisp
fraying ropes knotted and drawn tight
the wood stacked hyperboloid
pray tell how is this just
a torch starts kindling crackle
to the fear driven spectacle
firelight begins to grow
shining eyes flash and glisten
the seekers of proof
under veil of cloth
the whole town awash with guilt
thick smoke ventures forth
consuming all there
I prefer to hold you close
to the cries of witch
and join with you
amongst the stars

On the air.

feather on the air
omit by and large
a breadcrumb on the ground
in significance
shine on emerald tip

message carried on the wind
tethered with cotton thread
guidance in tow
the rings traverse
whisper to your friends

Hours past.

one mind, one cell
one cell, three prisons
communication, yes
hours past
connected, no

one bind, one rule
one rule, three lights
assimilation, yes
hours past
substantiated, no

About the author

Caley Dent was born in 1987 in Lower Hutt, Wellington, New Zealand.

Here he is home and has a successful career in the manufacturing sector.

Artistically Caley has always stayed true to his heart for expression whether it be through drawing, painting, band performance, solo recording artist, designer and now for the first time sharing his writing.